# CHILD SEXUAL ABUSE

# Framework for a Church Response

*Report of the*
*Irish Catholic Bishops' Advisory Committee*
*on Child Sexual Abuse by Priests and Religious*

## VERITAS

First published 1996 by
Veritas Publications
7-8 Lower Abbey Street
Dublin 1

ISBN 1 85390 325 6

Design by Bill Bolger
Printed in Ireland by Betaprint, Dublin

# Members of the Advisory Committee

Sr Éilís Bergin pbvm
Manager, St Bernard Residential Homes, Fethard, Co. Tipperary

Rev Frank Buckley
Dioceses of Cork and Ross

Ms Margaret Burns
Administrator, The Council for Social Welfare

Rev Damian Byrne op
Conference of Religious of Ireland

Mr Jim Cantwell
Director, Catholic Press and Information Office

Sr Geraldine Fitzgerald lcm
Member of Executive, Conference of Religious of Ireland

Most Rev Laurence Forristal
Bishop of Ossory, Chairman

Mr Edward Gleeson
Solicitor, Dublin

Mr Ted Jones
Solicitor, Belfast

Rev Lomán Mac Aodha ofm
National Conference of Priests of Ireland

Dr Imelda Ryan
Director, St Louise's Child Sexual Abuse Assessment and Treatment
Service, Dublin

Monsignor Alex Stenson
Professor of Canon Law, Holy Cross College, Clonliffe, Dublin

Dr Patrick Walsh
Director of Psychological Services, St John of God Order

# The Work of the Advisory Committee

The Advisory Committee which prepared this report was convened in March 1994, at the request of the Irish Catholic Bishops' Conference, under the chairmanship of Bishop Laurence Forristal, Bishop of Ossory. It first met on 27 April 1994.

The terms of reference of the Advisory Committee were:

> to consider and advise on an appropriate response by the Catholic Church in Ireland where there is an accusation, suspicion or knowledge of a priest or religious having sexually abused a child;

> to identify guidelines for Church policy in this area and suggest a set of procedures to be followed in these circumstances.

In the course of its deliberations, the Advisory Committee had the benefit of having the views and advice of individuals, including victims of abuse, and organisations with experience and expertise in relation to child sexual abuse.

During January and February 1995 the Advisory Committee held a series of listening days to hear the views of organisations in the statutory and voluntary sectors involved in child protection and welfare. (A list of these organisations is provided in Appendix 1.)

The Advisory Committee is most grateful to all these individuals and groups whose contribution to its work helped greatly in deepening its understanding of the issues involved.

Progress reports on the work of the Advisory Committee were made at each meeting of the Bishops' Conference over the period the Committee met, and on three occasions representatives of the Committee discussed with the Bishops' Conference the development of the Committee's thinking.

On a number of occasions the Advisory Committee met with and heard the views of religious superiors through the Conference of Religious of Ireland.

The Advisory Committee is most grateful for the generous assistance it received from bishops and their representatives in Britain, Canada and the United States.

Finally, the Advisory Committee expresses gratitude to the following who assisted in its work:

Rev Austin Flannery OP
Ms Maria Gilchrist
Mr Brian Matthews
Ms Nora Murphy
Most Rev Donal Murray
Most Rev Dermot O'Mahony
Ms Máire Ní Chearbhaill
Rev Myles Rearden CM
Rev Stephen Rossetti
Rev Osmund Slevin CP
Ms Carol Stanton

The Advisory Committee thanks also the President and staff of Holy Cross College, Clonliffe, for providing a meeting-place for the Committee and for their hospitality.

# Contents

# Foreword

On behalf of the Irish Bishops' Conference and the Conference of Religious of Ireland we welcome the report of the Bishops' Advisory Committee and we recommend it to individual dioceses and congregations as a framework for addressing the issue of child sexual abuse by priests and religious.

The Church has always had its limitations and sinfulness but child sexual abuse by priests and religious is one of the saddest manifestations of this reality. Such exploitation of the vulnerability of children is a betrayal of trust of the gravest kind.

We express our shame and sorrow that such incidents of abuse have occurred. On behalf of bishops, priests and religious we apologise to all who have suffered because of sexual abuse inflicted on them by priests and religious.

We recognise the hurt and sense of isolation which those who have been victims of child sexual abuse by priests and religious have experienced. As the Advisory Committee's report properly declares, those who have suffered abuse and their families should have the first call on the Church's pastoral concern.

The report recognises the paramount need to safeguard the welfare of children. It emphasises the need for a strong commitment to prevention through a range of measures to reduce the risk of such abuse in the future.

Catholics throughout Ireland have been hurt in recent times by the particular evil of child sexual abuse by priests and religious. Low morale, a sense of isolation, confusion, pain and anger are being experienced in the Church community.

Truly the whole Church has suffered. It is our hope that through the implementation of the recommendations in this report the process of restoring confidence can begin.

We are mindful also of those priests and religious who have offended. As members of our Church family they need our pastoral concern and care. We also remember the hurt to their families who have particularly experienced distress and shame.

This document is far from being the final word on how to address the issues which have been raised. In common with others in society the Church must constantly seek ways to improve its response to this grave wrong, the sexual abuse of children.

Our hope for the future is that the Church, through its own vigorous efforts and in collaboration with others who are working in the field of child protection, will play its full part in safeguarding the welfare of all children.

Cahal Cardinal Daly                                   John Byrne, OSA
President                                                      President
Irish Catholic Bishops' Conference    Conference of Religious of Ireland

12 December 1995

# Chapter 1

# A Church Response to Child Sexual Abuse

A Church response to child sexual abuse by priests and religious must be founded on an acknowledgment of the wrong which has been done to those who have suffered abuse. It must be informed by an understanding of the hurt which such abuse imposes and of the long-term harm it may cause. It must also be based on a recognition of the need for the Church to do all that it can towards healing the hurt and repairing the harm.

The sexual abuse of children is a grave violation of their right to bodily integrity and an invasion of their right to physical and emotional privacy. It represents an interference with their right to enjoy physical and mental health and with their right to grow and develop in an environment which recognises their inherent dignity and worth and which is conducive to the realisation of their full potential.

All child abuse, but particularly child sexual abuse, is a betrayal of a trust given to those who have a responsibility to safeguard the well-being of the children with whom they are in contact, however temporary that contact may be.

This betrayal of trust is compounded when the person who abuses is expected to behave according to clearly defined moral standards.

Child sexual abuse by priests and religious is a betrayal of their calling to serve others; it is a betrayal too of the Christian community which has entrusted them with particular authority and responsibility.

Instead of their special position in the Church being a means through which God's care for his people is revealed, priests and religious who sexually abuse children take advantage of that position to gratify their own desires and sense of power.

## The Effects of Child Sexual Abuse

The negative impact of sexual abuse on children should never be underestimated or minimised. Such abuse has the potential to affect the child victim physically, emotionally and spiritually, both in the short and long term. As well as the possibility of direct physical effects from the abuse itself, confusion can be created in the child victim about sexual norms and standards, leading to blurring of role boundaries. The child's emotional well-being may also be affected, whereby feelings of guilt and shame are engendered in the child, leading to a loss of a sense of self-worth, to a development of a low self-esteem and to an impaired ability to trust. Awareness and acknowledgement, at an early stage, that a child has been abused allows for appropriate intervention to help the child victim deal with the abuse experience.

If a child's abuse is not revealed and if appropriate help is not provided, the effects of that abuse can be long-lasting and can contribute to a variety of difficulties in adult life, including emotional, relationship and sexual problems. Even in adulthood, victims may feel stigmatised by having been abused in childhood. They may experience a deep sense of isolation. While needing the care and support of others, they may feel unable to reveal the fact that they have been abused even to close family or friends, fearing that their revelations may be disbelieved or not met with understanding.

A particular effect of abuse by a priest or religious is the harm which may be done to the person's religious faith. The shattering of trust by a priest or religious who abuses may destroy the person's trust in the Church and confidence in its ministers. Distrust of priests may result in the experiencing of significant difficulties in participating in the Eucharist and receiving the other sacraments. Indeed, the victim may feel unable to continue to be a member of the Church. Abuse may even damage or destroy belief in God.

## A Response by Church Authorities to those who have been Abused by Priests or Religious

Child sexual abuse does not reveal itself easily, nor do children make disclosures readily and openly. Children may feel trapped by the context and the nature of the relationship surrounding the abuse. They may be sensitive to the disruption they fear will follow their disclosure. Some children, therefore, never talk about their abuse experience. Others may not feel capable of doing so until well into adult life.

Those victims who come forward to Church authorities to talk about their abuse experiences need to be listened to, heard and have their experiences acknowledged in a caring, sensitive manner. Every effort should be made to reach an understanding of the impact of the abuse experience on the victim and his or her family because family members may also be affected by what has occurred. Families can feel that the integrity of the family unit has been damaged. They also may be confused, hurt and angry. They may experience a deep sense of betrayal, not only by the priest or religious who has abused, but by the whole institution which that person is seen to represent.

It is the victims of abuse and their families who must have first call on the Church's pastoral concern. The response of Church authorities to the needs of the victim and the victim's family must be sensitive to their wishes. In this regard, victims and their families should be assisted in gaining access to the counselling services that are available and accessible to them. If such services are not available, the Church should be willing to assist victims in obtaining the help they require. Furthermore, just as the Church throughout its history has provided services where these were absent or inadequate, so now it should be prepared to take initiatives, in co-operation with the statutory authorities, to set up therapeutic services which would be open to all victims of child sexual abuse.

The Church should be sensitive to the need which may exist to extend its care and concern for those who have suffered abuse and their families beyond the initial response which follows disclosure. If, as a result of abuse, people experience difficulties with regard to religious faith and practice, the Church has a particular responsibility to address these concerns with sensitivity and respect. It must do all that it can to afford the person who has been abused, and his or her family, the opportunity to experience the hope of new life and the possibility of change and renewal – even from the depths of pain and despair – which are at the heart of the Gospel message.

## The Protection of Children

The Church, as part of the community, shares the responsibility of ensuring that children are protected from abuse in all its forms.

From what is known of patterns of abusive behaviour, and the secrecy with which the person who abuses will manage to surround his or her abuse, there must always be a concern following an allegation of sexual abuse that other children may have been or may be still at risk of being abused. Church authorities therefore have an obligation to do all within their power to ensure that the risk of further abuse is minimised.

Church authorities also have a responsibility to create an open, understanding environment, whereby those who have suffered abuse will be enabled to disclose their experiences in the expectation of a sensitive and caring response. Education programmes have an essential part to play in the creation of that environment.

## Legal Framework

A Church response to child sexual abuse by priests and religious must accord with the legal framework in society for the investigation and prosecution of criminal offences and for ensuring the protection and welfare of children.

It is vital that Church authorities, and in particular those responsible for implementing procedures in dioceses and institutes of consecrated life or societies of apostolic life,* act in a spirit of co-operation with the civil authorities in their local area.

In responding to complaints of child sexual abuse, Church authorities must also act in accordance with the requirements of the Code of Canon Law and must respect the rights and uphold the safeguards afforded in that Code both to those who complain of abuse and to those who are accused.

---

* The term 'religious congregation' is henceforth used in this document to denote institutes of consecrated life or societies of apostolic life.

The Church has its own inherent right to constrain with penal sanctions its members, including priests and religious, who commit offences. These penal sanctions are clearly indicated in the Code of Canon Law (cf. c. 1311ff).

## Priests and Religious who are Accused of Child Sexual Abuse

A Church response to an allegation of child sexual abuse against a priest or religious must include respect for the rights of the person who has been accused. In particular, with due regard to the paramount need to protect children, care should be taken that the good name and reputation of a priest or religious who is accused is not unjustly tarnished. The fundamental presumption of innocence must be upheld and respected, unless the contrary has been established.

Careful attention must be given also to the spiritual and emotional well-being of the accused person. This must extend throughout the period of the investigation of an allegation and beyond whatever determination is made in regard to it.

Further, if it is found that an accusation is without foundation, extreme care is to be taken that the person wrongly accused is completely reinstated in good standing and that all blot or stain is entirely removed from his or her character and good name.

In cases where a priest or religious has been found to have abused, some people may feel that any continued care and concern for the abuser is misplaced. This feeling is understandable, given the gravity of child sexual abuse in terms of its violation of the abused person's rights and the danger that its effects may have long-term consequences for his or her well-being.

The knowledge that offenders may, even after the discovery of their abuse, continue to offend, might seem to justify an approach where the only concern is to punish and to ensure that there is no possibility of re-offending. The impulse to exclude those who abuse from society is very strong; indeed in many respects sexual abusers are treated as outcasts of society.

But priests and religious who offend are members of a Church founded on a Gospel message of love and forgiveness; this means that those who have offended can be helped to hope for and work towards healing and regeneration in their lives.

The hope of renewal and reform should mean that offenders should be supported in whatever efforts they make to effect a change in their behaviour which would enable them to live a life free of abuse. The offering of therapeutic help to offenders is vital towards assisting them cease their abusive behaviour. It is thus an important element in the prevention of abuse and the protection of children.

## Other Pastoral Considerations

An accusation that a priest or religious has sexually abused a child will usually come as an enormous shock to his or her family, close relatives and friends, to present and past colleagues, and to the parishes or communities in which he or she has worked. They are likely to have great difficulty in coming to terms with the possibility that someone whom they have known, trusted and respected or loved could be responsible for such behaviour. They may feel dismay, disappointment and a deep sense of betrayal if an allegation proves to be well-founded.

Church authorities must recognise the particular needs of these individuals and communities. In so far as is possible, they should respond, at an appropriate time, to the need for information concerning the allegation and the action being taken in response to it. This must be done within the requirement that the right of victims to privacy be safeguarded and the rights in law of the person who is accused be respected. There must also be other efforts to respond pastorally to the particular needs of these individuals and communities who may be deeply, if indirectly, hurt by sexual abuse by priests and religious.

## The Impact of the Revelations of Child Sexual Abuse

The sexual abuse of children by priests and religious has shocked and angered Church members and Irish society generally. A debt of gratitude is owed, however, to those who have had the courage to come forward and reveal the abuse they have suffered. Their courage has resulted in a breaking of the secrecy which is a particular feature of child sexual abuse. The greater degree of openness which now surrounds the issue means that other people who have suffered abuse but have kept it secret may now feel enabled to come forward.

The revelations about the sexual abuse of children by priests and religious have had an immense impact on the Catholic Church in Ireland and have provoked a crisis of faith and confidence among many of its members. While the vast majority of priests and religious have not been responsible for the sexual abuse of children, they have, as a result of the actions of those of their colleagues who have abused, experienced a lessening in morale and a diminution in the trust and esteem accorded to them. Confidence and trust need to be re-built; a coherent and effective response by Church authorities to the problem of child sexual abuse by priests and religious is an important element in that process.

There must be hope that this time of crisis may be also a time of opportunity for renewal and that from the current upheaval a better Church will emerge. However, this will happen only if its members – all its members – work with considerable energy and commitment. There must not be any complacent belief that the time of crisis will pass, after which, and without any special effort on anyone's part, life will be back to normal again.

The necessary renewal will involve a close working together of all within the Church. The greater degree of collaboration and shared responsibility required in the future will place significant demands not just on those who occupy leadership positions but on all members of the Church.

Such co-responsibility will be particularly required if there is to be an adequate response to the needs of victims of child sexual abuse, their families, and the needs also of individuals and communities affected by such abuse.

As part of the renewal required within the Church, all its adult members need to examine their attitudes towards and perceptions of children. This should lead to a deepening in the understanding of and respect for the rights of children and young people – not only to care and protection but to participate, as members, in the life of the Church in accordance with their age and capacity.

By exemplifying respect for the dignity and rights of children in its institutions and practices, the Church can effectively play its part in helping to create a society in which the needs and rights of all children are recognised and respected.

### The Advisory Committee's Report

The purpose of this document is to provide information and guidance which will assist Church authorities make an appropriate and effective response to the problem of child sexual abuse by priests and religious.

The Advisory Committee suggests that the following eight guidelines to action should underlie that response:

- The safety and welfare of children should be the first and paramount consideration following an allegation of child sexual abuse.

- A prompt response should be given to all allegations of child sexual abuse.

- In all instances where it is known or suspected that a priest or religious has sexually abused a child, the matter should be reported to the civil authorities.

- Care should be given to the emotional and spiritual well-being of those who have suffered abuse and their families.

- There should be immediate consideration, following a complaint, of all child protection issues which arise, including whether the accused priest or religious should continue in ministry during the investigation.

- The rights under natural justice, civil law and canon law of an accused priest or religious should be respected.

- An appropriate pastoral response to the parish and wider community should be provided, with due regard to the right of privacy of those directly involved, and to the administration of justice.

- Adequate positive steps should be taken to restore the good name and reputation of a priest or religious who has been wrongly accused of child sexual abuse.

The Advisory Committee is conscious that sections of its report, detailing the steps involved in the proposed procedures for responding to complaints of child sexual abuse, may seem bureaucratic in tone. However unavoidable this may be in producing a set of procedures, the response itself must not be bureaucratic. Those whose task it will be to put into practice procedures for a response must be conscious always of the hurt which has been experienced by those who have suffered abuse and the central requirement that any response on the part of the Church to their complaint must contribute to the process of healing that hurt.

While it is hoped that this document is potentially a useful aid to responding to the problem of child sexual abuse by priests and religious, its effectiveness in practice depends on those who have the authority to implement its proposals displaying a strong willingness and commitment to do so.

# Chapter 2

## Reporting of Child Sexual Abuse

### 2.1 Definition of Child Sexual Abuse

2.1.1 Sexual offences against minors are defined under statute in both the Republic of Ireland and Northern Ireland. However, neither legislators nor the courts have adopted an all-encompassing definition of child sexual abuse. The definition of child sexual abuse adopted by The Law Reform Commission,[1] for the purpose of a proposed mandatory reporting law,[2] is set forth below. The definition, while not inclusive of all sexual offences, clearly outlines the behaviour with which this document is concerned.

     *i.    Intentional touching of the body of a child for the purpose of the sexual arousal or sexual gratification of the child or the person;*

     *ii.   intentional masturbation in the presence of a child;*

     *iii.  intentional exposure of the sexual organs of a person or any other sexual act intentionally performed in the presence of a child for the purpose of sexual arousal or gratification of the older person or as an expression of aggression, threat or intimidation towards the child; and*

     *iv.  sexual exploitation, which includes permitting, encouraging or requiring a child to solicit for or to engage in prostitution or other sexual acts as referred to above with the accused or any other person, persons, animal or thing or engaging in the recording (on video-tape, film, audio-tape or other temporary*

---

1. This definition was originally proposed by the Western Australia Task Force and is quoted in The Law Reform Commission, *Report on Child Sexual Abuse*, Dublin: The Law Reform Commission, 1990, p.8.
2. A summary of the existing law in relation to the reporting of sexual abuse of children, in the Republic of Ireland and in Northern Ireland, is contained in Appendix 2.

*or permanent material), posing, modelling or performing of any act involving the exhibition of a child's body for the purpose of sexual gratification of an audience or for the purpose of any other sexual act referred to in subparagraphs (i) and (iii) above.*

2.1.2 While the criminal code contains specific offences at varying ages of childhood, it is recommended that for the purpose of this document a child be defined as a person under the age of eighteen years.

2.1.3 A summary of the legal framework within which child sexual abuse is dealt with in the Republic of Ireland and in Northern Ireland is provided in Appendix 3.

## 2.2 Recommended Reporting Policy

2.2.1 In all instances where it is known or suspected that a child has been, or is being, sexually abused by a priest or religious the matter should be reported to the civil authorities. Where the suspicion or knowledge results from the complaint of an adult of abuse during his or her childhood, this should also be reported to the civil authorities.

2.2.2 The report should be made without delay to the senior ranking police officer for the area in which the abuse is alleged to have occurred. Where the suspected victim is a child, or where a complaint by an adult gives rise to child protection questions, the designated person within the appropriate health board[3]/health and social services board[4] should also be informed. A child protection question arises, in the case of a complaint by an adult, where an accused priest or religious holds or has held a position which has afforded him or her unsupervised access to children.

2.2.3 The Advisory Committee recognises that this recommended reporting policy may cause difficulty in that some people who

---

3. Republic of Ireland
4. Northern Ireland

come to the Church with complaints of current or past child sexual abuse by a priest or religious seek undertakings of confidentiality. They are concerned to protect the privacy of that abuse of which even their immediate family members may not be aware. Their primary reason in coming forward may be to warn Church authorities of a priest or religious who is a risk to children.

2.2.4   The recommended reporting policy may deter such people from coming forward or may be perceived by those who do come forward as an insensitive and heavy-handed response by Church authorities. This is particularly so where the complaint relates to incidents of abuse many years earlier.

2.2.5   Nonetheless, undertakings of absolute confidentiality should not be given but rather the information should be expressly received within the terms of this reporting policy and on the basis that only those who need to know will be told.[5]

2.2.6   In making its recommendations in regard to reporting, the Advisory Committee considers to be paramount the safety and protection of children and the need to prevent, where possible, further abuse.

---

5. The recommended reporting policy does not apply to the relationship between penitent and confessor; the seal of confession is, of course, inviolable. (Cf. the Code of Canon Law, c. 983.)

# Chapter 3

# Structures for a Church Response

3.1     Each diocese and each religious congregation should adopt a protocol for responding effectively to complaints of child sexual abuse by priests or religious.[6]

3.2     The protocol, once adopted by a diocesan bishop or competent religious superior, in accordance with the congregation's Constitutions, should be communicated to all the priests and religious of the diocese or religious congregation and be available to the public.

3.3     The protocol should embody and reflect the eight guidelines to action already outlined:

•       The safety and welfare of children should be the first and paramount consideration following an allegation of child sexual abuse.

•       A prompt response should be given to all allegations of child sexual abuse.

•       In all instances where it is known or suspected that a priest or religious has sexually abused a child, the matter should be reported to the civil authorities.

•       Care should be given to the emotional and spiritual well-being of those who have suffered abuse and their families.

•       There should be immediate consideration, following a complaint, of all child protection issues which arise, including whether the accused priest or religious should continue in ministry during the investigation.

---

6. The protocol of a diocese or religious congregation should reflect obligations under both civil and canon law.

- The rights under natural justice, civil law and canon law of an accused priest or religious should be respected.

- An appropriate pastoral response to the parish and wider community should be provided, with due regard to the right of privacy of those directly involved, and to the administration of justice.

- Adequate positive steps should be taken to restore the good name and reputation of a priest or religious who has been wrongly accused of child sexual abuse.

3.4    The uniqueness of each complaint demands that judgement and discretion should be carefully exercised in the implementation of each phase of the protocol.

3.5    It is further incumbent upon those who perform functions under the protocol to carefully respect the privacy of all parties in an accusation, in order that the right of each individual to his or her good name and reputation is upheld.

3.6    The bishop or religious superior should conduct a regular review of the manner in which the protocol is operating so that whatever needs to be changed may be promptly identified and the requisite amendments made. This review should be conducted in consultation with those who exercise functions under the protocol.

3.7    When a complaint of child sexual abuse is made against a priest or religious, the bishop or religious superior, in fulfilment of pastoral responsibilities and obligations under canon law, must have careful regard to the well-being of all those who are or may be affected. In particular, the bishop or religious superior should consider the needs of those who may have suffered abuse and their families, of the accused priest or religious and his or her family, of the parish or other place of ministry in which the accused person has served, and of the wider Church community. The bishop or religious superior should be available to meet pastorally those who have suffered abuse and their families.

3.8     If any person holding a position within the structure envisaged below is himself or herself accused of child sexual abuse, steps should be taken to appoint a substitute or otherwise alter the procedures as appropriate.

3.9     Because of the obligations of the sacramental seal, no priest performing a function under the protocol should celebrate the Sacrament of Penance with an accused priest or religious.

## The Delegate

3.10    Each bishop or religious superior should appoint a Delegate to oversee and implement the adopted protocol and to have such additional responsibilities in relation to child sexual abuse as may be required. A deputy Delegate should also be appointed who would have the same duties and functions as the Delegate in the latter's absence or incapacity, or for any other sufficient reason.

3.11    The Delegate and deputy Delegate should be carefully chosen and should undergo training to ensure that they have the necessary skills, including an understanding of the dynamics of child sexual abuse, of its impact on victims, and of clinical and public policy developments in the area. They should also have an understanding of the implications an allegation has for the person who is accused.

3.12    The Delegate and deputy Delegate should be widely identified and known as such to facilitate easy access by all.

3.13    Every complaint of child sexual abuse against a priest or religious which is received, whether by a bishop or religious superior, a priest or other person, should be communicated to the appropriate Delegate.

## The Support Person

3.14    Each bishop or religious superior should appoint a specific person – the Support Person – to be available to those who allege that they have suffered abuse and their families. The role of this person will be to assist those wishing to make a complaint of child sexual abuse, to facilitate them in gaining access to information and help, and to represent their concerns on an ongoing basis. In larger dioceses and religious congregations there may be a need to have more than one person available to act in this capacity. The Support Person should receive appropriate training.

## The Adviser

3.15    Each bishop or religious superior should appoint an Adviser to be available to the accused priest or religious. The Adviser should have regard to all pastoral, legal and therapeutic issues arising for the accused priest or religious. The Adviser should receive appropriate training.

3.16    The accused priest or religious should be legally represented by a solicitor who is independent of the solicitor representing the diocese or religious congregation.

## The Advisory Panel

3.17    Each bishop or religious superior should appoint an Advisory Panel, the members of which will be available to offer advice on a confidential basis, collectively and in their respective disciplines, when required. The Panel should include lay people with qualities and expertise relevant to the issue of child sexual abuse. It is recommended that a child care professional, a canon lawyer and a civil lawyer be included in the membership of the Panel.

## Media Relations

3.18    Media relations on behalf of the diocese or religious congregation should be handled by an identified person who should have appropriate training. It is vital that the media response take fully into account:

*    the protection of the right of victims to privacy;

- the protection of the right of the accused to a fair trial – the right to a fair trial is the right to a trial in which prospective jurors are not potentially prejudiced by pre-trial publicity.

## *The General Functions of a Delegate*

3.19 The Delegate should be empowered and directed by the bishop or religious superior to respond immediately whenever a complaint of child sexual abuse against a priest or religious is received.

3.20 The Delegate should ensure that the protocol is implemented when a complaint of child sexual abuse is made against a priest or religious.

3.21 The Delegate should be responsible for ensuring that every complaint is recorded and carefully examined so that all pastoral, legal and canonical obligations may be identified and acted upon at the earliest time. The Delegate should have responsibility for the co-ordination of the response of the diocese or religious congregation to the complaint.

3.22 The Delegate should be familiar with the working arrangements of the civil authorities of the local area in the investigation of complaints of child sexual abuse and should be known to and liaise with their personnel who have responsibility for different aspects of child abuse allegations.

3.23 The Delegate should be conversant with the treatment facilities available to victims of child sexual abuse.

3.24 The Delegate should be familiar with the assessment and treatment facilities available to people accused of child sexual abuse.

3.25 The Delegate of each diocese or religious congregation should promote awareness and understanding of child sexual abuse among the priests of the diocese or members of the religious congregation.

# Chapter 4

## Procedure for Responding to Complaints

### 4.1    Making a Complaint

4.1.1    A person who wishes to bring a complaint of child sexual abuse against a priest or religious should contact the Delegate of the diocese or religious congregation to which the priest or religious belongs. The Delegate should be available to receive information about complaints without delay.

### 4.2    Receipt of a Complaint by a Priest or Religious other than the Delegate

4.2.1    A priest or religious other than the Delegate who is approached by an adult or a child who alleges child sexual abuse by a priest or religious should:

*where the complainant is an adult*

- listen carefully to that person;

- explain the procedure the diocese or religious congregation has put in place for dealing with complaints against priests or religious, including its policy on reporting to the civil authorities;

- offer to accompany the person in bringing the complaint to the Delegate;

- make a careful written record of what the complainant has alleged.

*where the complainant is a child*

- take what the child says seriously;

- reassure the child;

- listen carefully and attentively but under no circumstances ask leading questions;

- check with the child to ensure that what has been heard and understood accords with what the child actually said;

- make no promises which cannot be kept;

- accompany the child to his or her parent or guardian;

- tell the parent or guardian exactly what the child has said;

- explain to the parent or guardian the procedure the diocese or religious congregation has put in place for dealing with complaints against priests or religious, including its policy on reporting to the civil authorities;

- inform the Delegate of what has occurred and provide the Delegate with a precise written record of what the child has said, any views expressed by the child's parent or guardian about the matter, and of the steps taken.

4.2.2 It is envisaged that the response of the diocese or religious congregation to the complaint will thereafter be co-ordinated by the Delegate, who will also implement the reporting policy.

### 4.3 Receipt by the Delegate of Indirect Information about a Complaint

4.3.1 If a person other than a parent or guardian comes forward with an allegation that a third party has been sexually abused during childhood by a priest or religious, the Delegate should provide the person making the allegation with an explanation of Church procedures in these circumstances. The following information should be sought:

- the relationship of that person to the suspected victim;

- the source, manner and time of acquiring such knowledge;

- the name and age of the suspected victim, and other relevant information;

- the name of the accused priest or religious;

- the facts and circumstances of the allegation;

- whether the civil authorities have yet been made aware of the allegation.

4.3.2 Where the Delegate otherwise learns indirectly of a complaint of child sexual abuse against a priest or religious – if, for example, it becomes known that a police investigation is under way – the Delegate should endeavour to ascertain what is known of the accusation.

4.3.3 In all instances where indirect information is received, it will be the responsibility of the Delegate to co-ordinate a response to the situation so that all appropriate measures are promptly taken in accordance with the protocol.

## 4.4 Receipt by the Delegate of a Direct Complaint

4.4.1 The following assumes that the complainant is the parent or guardian of a child who alleges abuse, or an adult who alleges abuse during childhood.

4.4.2 It should at all times be remembered that the process of disclosure of child sexual abuse is painful, requiring very considerable courage on the part of a victim or his or her family.

4.4.3 In so far as is practicable, the Support Person[7] should be available from the beginning to provide assistance and information to the complainant and identify any therapeutic or other needs he or she might have.

4.4.4 The Delegate, on meeting the complainant, should explain the procedure of the diocese or religious congregation for responding to complaints of child sexual abuse against priests or religious and, in particular, point out that:

- The complainant should give consideration to reporting the complaint to the police and, as appropriate, to the health board/health and social services board. The complainant

7. Cf. 3.14.

should also be informed of the reporting policy of the diocese or religious congregation.

- Every effort will be made to safeguard confidentiality so that only those people who need to know will receive information about the complaint. However, no guarantee of absolute confidentiality can be given.

- In the Church, the specific rights and duties of priests or religious are such that where there is a complaint of child sexual abuse against a priest or religious, an enquiry into the complaint under canon law is required.[8] The future co-operation of the complainant will be sought in so far as it may be necessary. Care will be taken that such an enquiry will not interfere with or be prejudicial to the administration of justice in any state criminal investigation or civil suit.

4.4.5    The Delegate should ask the complainant to provide a detailed account of the wrongful acts alleged and their background and circumstances. The Delegate should carefully record what is said, and check with the complainant the accuracy of what has been recorded. Ample time must be given to this.

4.4.6    In addition, the Delegate should try to identify the wishes, intentions and expectations of the complainant, and should explain the role of the diocese or religious congregation in regard to the complaint and the context within which it must operate.

## 4.5    The Response to a Complaint

*Action by the Delegate*

4.5.1    Following receipt of the complaint, the Delegate should:

---

8. Cf. the Code of Canon Law, Book VII, Part IV, cc. 1717 ff. (for Religious cf. Book II, Part III, cc. 694 ff.); Canadian Conference of Catholic Bishops, *From Pain to Hope*, Ottawa: Canadian Conference of Catholic Bishops, 1992, Appendix 3, pp. 73-76; J. Alesandro, 'Dismissal from the Clerical State in Cases of Sexual Misconduct', *CLSA Proceedings*, 56, 1994, pp. 40-57; *Canonical Delicts Involving Sexual Misconduct and Dismissal from the Clerical State*, Washington, DC: National Conference of Catholic Bishops, 1995; The Canon Law Society of Great Britain and Ireland, *The Canon Law, Letter and Spirit*, Dublin: Veritas Publications, 1995, pp. 389-395 and pp. 953-960; Jordan Hite TOR, Sharon Holland IHM and Daniel Ward OSB (eds.), *Religious Institutes, Secular Institutes, Societies of Apostolic Life, A Handbook of Canons 573-746*, Collegeville: Liturgical Press, 1985.

- implement the reporting policy outlined;[9]

- inform the bishop or religious superior of the complaint;

- identify the present and previous appointments of the accused priest or religious;

- liaise with the Support Person;[10]

- alert the Adviser[11] to be on standby, without identifying the accused priest or religious;

- ensure the availability of the Advisory Panel[12] if required, and convene the Advisory Panel at an appropriate time;

- conduct an interview with the accused priest or religious at an appropriate time.

*Action by the Support Person*

4.5.2    The Support Person will be particularly attentive to the fact that some victims and their families may be reluctant to seek help and should consider, therefore, how any therapeutic or spiritual needs of a person who has suffered abuse may be met.

4.5.3    In addition, the Support Person should:

- consider any wishes of the complainant in regard to a pastoral response by the Church to his or her family;

- be available to the complainant throughout any investigation which may ensue, and thereafter as required;

- ensure that the complainant is kept informed of developments in regard to the complaint;

- represent the wishes and any therapeutic needs of the complainant to the Delegate as required;

---

9. Cf. 2.2.1-2.2.2.
10. Cf. 3.14.
11. Cf. 3.15.
12. Cf. 3.17.

- arrange, if considered helpful, a meeting between the complainant and the bishop or religious superior.

*Action by the Bishop or Religious Superior*

4.5.4   On hearing of the complaint from the Delegate, the bishop or religious superior will ensure that, where applicable, the requirements of c.1717 are fulfilled by appropriate decree.

4.5.5   The stages hereafter of this procedure assume that, if a decree under c. 1717 is made, the Delegate has been appointed to carry out the enquiry. If a person other than the Delegate is appointed, appropriate adjustment will be required to ensure that all of the objectives of the protocol are fulfilled.

4.5.6   The bishop or religious superior should enquire into the nature of the duties and activities of the accused priest or religious in his or her present and previous appointments. Other relevant background information should be sought and considered.

4.5.7   The bishop or religious superior should consider the child welfare implications of the complaint, having regard to the appointment(s) held by the person who has been accused.

4.5.8   The bishop or religious superior should, without delay, meet and inform the accused priest or religious that a complaint has been received and that it is being dealt with in accordance with the procedure of the diocese or religious congregation. He or she should request the accused person to meet the Delegate.

4.5.9   The bishop or religious superior should explain to the accused priest or religious the role of the Adviser[13] who is available to him or her.

4.5.10   The bishop or religious superior should assure the accused person of his or her availability and pastoral concern, which would also extend to members of the accused person's family.

---

13. Cf. 3.15.

*The Role of the Adviser after the Accused Person's Meeting with the Bishop or Religious Superior*

4.5.11   The Adviser will be particularly alert to the sense of isolation and vulnerability which an accused priest or religious may experience following an accusation of this nature. He or she will:

- be available after the accused person's meeting with the bishop or religious superior, and accompany the accused person, if so requested, to the meeting with the Delegate;

- inform the accused priest or religious of his or her rights both in civil and canon law.

*Meeting Between the Delegate and the Accused Priest or Religious*

4.5.12   Having followed the reporting policy outlined above, and being at all times careful not to interfere with any investigation by the civil authorities, an interview should be conducted as soon as possible by the Delegate with the accused priest or religious. The Adviser should normally be present at this interview. The Delegate should inform the accused priest or religious of the nature and detail of the complaint and the name of the complainant. The Delegate should point out that:

- the matter is being enquired into in accordance with canon law;[14]

- the accused person is not obliged, in law, to respond or to furnish evidence;

- the accused person is entitled to the assistance of civil and canonical legal advisers.

4.5.13   If the accused person wishes to speak freely to the Delegate, a careful contemporaneous note should be taken by the Delegate of what the accused person says in response to the complaint. This should be checked with the accused person for accuracy.

---

14. The accused priest or religious should be informed of the canonical procedures under which the enquiry is being conducted.

4.5.14 Where an accused priest or religious expresses the wish to consult with civil and canonical advisers before responding, arrangements should be made for a further meeting at which such advisers will be welcome to attend with the accused priest or religious.

4.5.15 It is important that the Delegate discuss with the accused person and his or her Adviser the question of obtaining spiritual and therapeutic support as may be considered appropriate.

*Ongoing Role of the Adviser*

4.5.16 Following on the meeting with the Delegate, it will be for the Adviser to:

- identify any therapeutic or other needs of the accused person and suggest how these may be met;

- consider the wishes of the accused person in regard to a pastoral response by the Church to his or her family;

- be available to the accused person throughout any investigation which may ensue, and thereafter as required;

- ensure the accused person is kept informed of developments in regard to the complaint;

- represent the needs and wishes of the accused person to the Delegate, as required.

## 4.6 The Report of the Delegate and Subsequent Action

4.6.1 The Delegate should, as soon as possible, make a report to the bishop or religious superior on the complaint made and the response of the accused priest or religious. In circumstances where a police investigation is under way, completion of a report may have to be deferred. Nonetheless, certain steps in canon law may require to be taken in order to safeguard the common good.[15]

4.6.2 The bishop or religious superior will determine, on receipt of the report of the Delegate, whether further enquiries are necessary to establish the facts of the complaint.

---

15. Cf. the Code of Canon Law, c. 223.

4.6.3 The bishop or religious superior should consult the Support Person and the Adviser in order to afford an opportunity for any representation on behalf of either the complainant or the accused priest or religious to be made.

4.6.4 The bishop or religious superior should then consider carefully the following:

- the complaint itself;

- the appropriateness of providing help, if needed, to a person making a complaint and to the family of the person;

- the appropriateness of the accused priest or religious continuing in his or her present pastoral assignment, having regard to the paramount need to protect children – care should be taken that a decision by a priest or religious to take leave of absence from a ministry will not be construed as denoting guilt on his or her part;

- how the right of the accused priest or religious to a fair trial on any criminal charge may be preserved, and his or her good name and reputation may be appropriately safeguarded;

- whether a specialist professional evaluation of the accused priest or religious should be sought at this stage;[16]

- the needs of a parish or other community where an accused priest or religious has served;

- the needs of the wider community including the appropriateness and timing of any public statement.

4.6.5 The bishop or religious superior should consult with the Advisory Panel in relation to all of the above matters. However, having had the benefit of the advice of the Panel, the bishop or religious superior should make his or her own determinations.

---

16. C.220 of the Code of Canon Law constitutes a limitation in regard to the use of experts in psychologically evaluating an accused person. Nevertheless, a bishop or religious superior, having received a Delegate's report (cf. c. 1717ff), could order a priest or religious under obedience to submit to the evaluation of experts. (Cf. Kevin W. Vann and James I. Donlon (eds.), *Roman Replies and CLSA Advisory Opinions 1995*, Washington DC: Canon Law Society of America, 1995, pp. 43-45.)

4.6.6   If the bishop or religious superior is satisfied that child sexual abuse has occurred, appropriate steps should be taken to ensure that the accused priest or religious does not remain in any pastoral appointment which affords access to children.

4.6.7   Where it is established that a priest or religious has offended, canon law indicates that before imposing ecclesiastical penalties, other means of correction or reproof should first be attempted.[17]

4.6.8   Should these means prove ineffective, canon law provides the bishop or religious superior with a range of options which may ultimately result in the penalty of dismissal from the clerical state or dismissal from the religious state.

4.6.9   In the consideration of steps which might be taken under canon law, the bishop or religious superior should consult closely with the canon lawyer who is a member of the Advisory Panel.

4.7     **Restoring the Reputation of a Priest or Religious Wrongly Accused**

4.7.1   Because an accused person is presumed innocent unless the contrary has been established, natural justice, civil law and canon law demand that he or she should not be punished on the basis of mere allegation. Where an allegation is not subsequently substantiated, a grave injustice will have been caused to the accused person.

4.7.2   If the civil authorities decide not to prosecute and the bishop or religious superior is satisfied after consideration of the facts and circumstances of the complaint that the priest or religious has been wrongly accused, appropriate steps should be taken to restore the good name of the priest or religious with those among whom it has been called into question, and to repair such harm and scandal as has been caused.

4.7.3   Where the allegation has been withdrawn and admitted to be false, similar steps should be taken as required.

---

17. Cf. the Code of Canon Law, c. 1341.

# Chapter 5

# Exchange of Information between Religious Congregations and Dioceses

5.1    Where a complaint has been made against a member of a religious congregation, the religious superior of the congregation should inform the bishop of the diocese in which the religious is living about the allegation – even if the person accused has no diocesan appointment in the diocese. The religious superior should also inform the bishop of the diocese in which the alleged wrongdoing occurred, if this is other than the diocese in which the accused person lives.

5.2    It is essential that the religious superior keep the bishop(s) informed of developments in regard to any particular complaint and of its final outcome.

5.3    In the case of a diocesan priest, the bishop of his diocese should ensure similar communication with dioceses in which the priest may, at any time, have served and with religious congregations with which he may have served.

5.4    Bishops should review their procedures for accepting priests or religious from elsewhere for any diocesan appointment, of whatever duration. This review should extend to the manner in which 'supply' arrangements are made at parochial level.

5.5    It is recommended that a system of formal referencing from the diocese or religious congregation of origin be implemented.[18]

5.6    This system of referencing should also form part of the procedure involved when a priest requests diocesan faculties.

5.7    Religious superiors should also review procedures for accepting

---

18. A sample form for such a procedure is provided in Appendix 4.

religious of their congregation coming from other countries to reside in an Irish community or to take up an appointment within the congregation. Clearance such as is suggested in 5.5 above should be sought and obtained.

# Chapter 6

# Parish and Local Community Issues

6.1     Where, following an allegation of child sexual abuse against a priest working in a parish appointment, the accused priest has requested leave of absence from the parish, or where this has been imposed,[19] the bishop should appoint a priest to replace him as soon as possible. He may have to appoint a parish administrator as an interim measure. The person appointed should be appropriately briefed.

6.2     The bishop should then provide the priests of the parish, and, where necessary, the priests of neighbouring parishes and former colleagues of the accused priest in previous appointments, with appropriate information. In so doing, he will have careful regard to the issue of privacy and the need to avoid any interference with the due administration of justice.

6.3     There is an understandable desire on the part of parishioners to know the facts and circumstances when a priest has been accused of child sexual abuse. Frequently, rumour and innuendo will follow an unexpected departure of a priest from a parish appointment. However, a public statement should be made only where the bishop is satisfied that the privacy of the suspected victim or victims will not be jeopardised and the right of the accused priest to a fair trial will not be placed at risk. It may be helpful to consult with the police or health board/health and social services board in this regard.

6.4     The absence of any statement at parish level may serve to heighten the concerns and fears of parents that their children may have been at risk of abuse. It is recommended that careful consultation should take place with the civil authorities in regard to how these concerns and fears might be addressed.

---

19. Leave of absence can be imposed under the terms of c. 1722 of the Code of Canon Law.

6.5     Subject to the constraints outlined above (cf. 6.3), the bishop should consult with his Advisory Panel and media spokesperson on the appropriateness, timing and content of a public statement.

6.6     The bishop should, at an appropriate time, make a pastoral visit to the parish or parishes affected, during which he should listen to and address, in so far as he may, the needs and concerns of the parishioners.

6.7     Based on the needs expressed by people during this visit, a programme of pastoral support and spiritual renewal for the parish or local Church community should be jointly prepared by the bishop, the local priests and pastoral council.

6.8     A spiritual retreat or mission designed to hear the concerns of the community, and to facilitate healing and reconciliation in the light of those concerns, might be arranged. Religious congregations with particular expertise in mission and retreat-giving should be invited to develop suitable programmes for this purpose.

# Chapter 7

# The Assessment and Treatment of Priests and Religious Accused of Child Sexual Abuse

## 7.1    Assessment

7.1.1    Assessment is a complex and specialised procedure which must be carried out by a multi-disciplinary team of clinicians, trained and experienced in assessing sexual deviancies, who work together to achieve a comprehensive understanding of the accused person. The validity and reliability of assessment will depend on the clinicians having access to all available information.

7.1.2    The assessment clinicians must undertake to discuss their findings with the person assessed and present this person with a comprehensive report. The assessment should be conducted on the clear understanding that the report will be made available to the bishop or religious superior of the person assessed.[20]

7.1.3    A comprehensive assessment of the person alleged to have abused requires considerable time, during which information can be gathered and cross-checked. Depending on the mental state of the person being assessed, the level of risk, the nature of the allegations, his or her location and the availability of services, this may be carried out on an out-patient or an in-patient basis.

## 7.2    Treatment

7.2.1    Where, as a result of assessment, an accused person is deemed to require treatment, it is recommended that the opportunity for treatment be offered to him or her.

7.2.2    While the effectiveness of treatment programmes must be regarded with some caution, certain offenders do appear to benefit from particular types of intervention. The most effective programmes combine individual and group methods which

20. Cf. footnote 16.

focus on the pattern of abusive behaviour and the cognitive distortions and deviant fantasies which support the abuse. The success of these programmes is dependent on the capacity of the abuser to empathise with victims, the development of the ability to establish and maintain appropriate interpersonal relationships, and compliance with a system of monitoring to prevent relapse.

7.2.3 In order to benefit from treatment, the offender must acknowledge that he or she has committed an offence and be prepared to accept responsibility for it. The offender must be brought to see the abuse as a grave problem not only for the victim(s) but also for him or herself, and must be willing to enter into and participate actively in the treatment.

7.2.4 The treatment programme should provide a structured environment which allows for a detailed observation of the person sent for treatment as well as an opportunity to determine the ability of the person to begin a process of change in his or her life. One of the aims of such a programme should be to facilitate disclosure and to act against the denial and minimisation which are characteristic of the abuser. The treatment programme should also strive to provide a supportive environment in which strategies designed to prevent relapse can be developed and practised and a change in lifestyle for the abuser can be consolidated.

7.2.5 Because the needs of offenders are complex, multi-disciplinary and multi-agency collaboration is essential if offenders are to be offered effective treatment and management. There is need to expand existing programmes for abusers and to develop new services, including residential services. The Church should consider how it can co-operate with statutory and voluntary agencies towards the provision of such additional services.

7.3 Following Assessment and Treatment

7.3.1 Because the sexual abuse of children is a grave breach of the sacred trust vested in a priest or religious the options for the future of those who offend in this way are greatly curtailed. Each situation will be different and will require a degree of flexibility and adaptation.

7.3.2　Where the offender is a contemplative religious it may be possible for him or her to continue living a full religious life in Community, without being permitted access to children.

7.3.3　Other forms of religious life may also offer possibilities to a religious who has offended for living a fruitful, if monitored, religious life focused on the internal life of the Community.

7.3.4　A religious superior may determine, in a particular case, that the imposition of an ecclesiastical penalty is required, in accordance with canon law.

7.3.5　A religious who has offended may decide to depart permanently from the religious life.

7.3.6　In relation to diocesan priests who have offended, the options would include:

- retirement under monitored conditions;

- laicisation sought by the priest;

- a canonical determination by the bishop which may involve the imposition of ecclesiastical penalties, not excluding dismissal from the clerical state, in accordance with canon law.

7.3.7　In exceptional cases, it may be possible to assign a priest or religious who has offended to an appointment of limited ministry which would not involve unsupervised contact with children. A decision to make such an appointment could be taken only after careful consultation with professional clinicians, trained and experienced in assessing sexual deviancies, and when morally certain that this re-assignment would not present a danger to children. The protection and welfare of children must be always the paramount and overriding consideration in arriving at a decision.

7.3.8    Before arriving at a decision to appoint a priest or religious who has offended to any limited ministry, the bishop or religious superior should be satisfied that the following conditions are met:

- completion of a comprehensive assessment and treatment programme with a favourable opinion on the person's suitability for the proposed assignment;

- a positive recommendation from the Advisory Panel in regard to the proposed assignment;

- the elapse of a period of time after treatment during which his or her behaviour has been observed;

- the priest or religious permits disclosure of his or her past abusing to those who will be in authority in the proposed assignment and such others as they consider need to know;

- the priest or religious will avoid unsupervised contact with children, and the assignment does not afford such contact;

- a system of individual monitoring has been put in place which ensures supervision and accountability;

- an after-care programme involving individual and group therapy has been arranged to provide continuing support and guidance.

7.3.9    Having been satisfied that such a limited assignment to ministry is possible, the bishop or religious superior should make the assignment by way of a Precept. This would contain the following:

- the place of residence of the priest or religious and the terms of the limited assignment;

- the conditions of supervision;

- the requirement that the priest or religious participate in a recovery support group and therapy;

- the requirement that the priest or religious should avoid being alone with children;

- the acceptance of the disclosure of his or her condition to those in authority at the place of assignment and such others as they consider need to know;

- a condition that violation of the Precept would result in his or her removal from the assignment.

7.3.10 The terms of the Precept should be agreed to by the priest or religious and this would be recorded. The bishop or religious superior should review the assignment with all parties concerned on a regular basis.

# Selection and Formation for the Diocesan Priesthood and for the Religious Life

## 8.1 Selection of Candidates

*In all recent statements on priesthood and religious life the Church has repeatedly stressed the importance of maturity in people who enter formation programmes for the priesthood and the religious life. Pope Paul VI emphasised the importance of an appropriate maturity at the beginning of formation and traced most difficulties in formation to lack of such maturity.[21] In his exhortation after the 1990 Synod on the Formation of Priests, Pope John Paul II suggested a sufficient period of preparation for candidates before formal training begins.[22]*

8.1.1   Selection and screening of candidates are of the greatest importance. Candidates should have proper motivation, an adequate knowledge of the faith, and a commitment to Christian values and living. It is important that they also have an affective maturity which includes reasonable awareness and acceptance of their sexuality, and an ability to relate to all those to whom they will be expected to minister – both adults and children.

8.1.2   The pre-admission programme suggested by Pope John Paul II in his post-Synod document on priestly formation[23] is necessary for at least some, if not all, candidates. One of the essential purposes of this programme would be to establish if candidates are able to relate adequately to their peers and others.

8.1.3   The selection process should be determined by the signs of a real vocation and not by any shortage of candidates for the priesthood or the religious life.

---

21. Vatican II, *Decree on the Up-to-Date Renewal of Religious Life*, 28 October 1965, in Austin Flannery OP (General Editor), *Vatican II: The Conciliar and Post-Conciliar Documents* (new revised edition), Dublin: Dominican Publications, 1992, p. 639.
22. *Pastores Dabo Vobis: Apostolic Exhortation of His Holiness John Paul II on the Formation of Priests in the Circumstances of the Present Day*, London: Catholic Truth Society, 1992, n. 62.
23. The same paragraph.

8.1.4    The selection of candidates for priesthood and religious life needs to be seen as an integral process involving the vocational director, the interview board and the bishop or religious superior.

8.1.5    The screening of candidates should normally include a full psychological assessment by an experienced psychologist[24] 'well-versed in and supportive of the Church's expectations of candidates for the priesthood or religious life, especially in regard to celibacy'.[25]

8.1.6    Oral references from responsible people who have known candidates over a long time are also important aids to the selection of candidates. Good examination results, along with school or other references, cannot be considered adequate by themselves.

8.1.7    The admission of candidates to seminary or religious formation must be the joint responsibility of the bishop or religious superior and formation personnel.

## 8.2    The Seminary and Religious House of Studies

*'The integral formation of a person has a physical, moral, intellectual and spiritual dimension.'*[26] *While intellectual formation is likely to be adequately covered, it is vitally important to maintain a balance between all four elements. Above all, what is needed is 'a true love and a sincere respect for the person who, in conditions which are very personal, is proceeding towards the priesthood or religious profession'.*[27]

8.2.1    An atmosphere should be created in seminaries and other houses of formation such that candidates, while being challenged, can be open about their inner struggle towards fuller maturity. Formators, while being companions to the candidates in their pilgrimage of faith, will need to recognise that they themselves are engaged in the same struggle. The openness which this

24. Cf. footnote 16; see the Code of Canon Law, c. 220 and c. 642.
25. Cf. *Program for Priestly Formation* (fourth edition), Washington DC: National Conference of Catholic Bishops, 1993, n. 518.
26. Congregation for Institutes of Consecrated Life and Societies of Apostolic Life, *Directives on Formation in Religious Institutes*, Rome: Vatican Polyglot Press, 1990, n. 34.
27. *Pastores Dabo Vobis*, n. 61.

process will require both of candidates and formators calls for considerable sensitivity and trust.

8.2.2 Formation is progressive, and must be evenly balanced between the human, spiritual, intellectual and pastoral. The whole process of formation of candidates for the priesthood and religious life should foster an integration of human sexuality and the development of healthy human relationships within the context of celibate living.

8.2.3 Lay men and women should be involved in the training of priests and religious.[28] All formators – priests, religious and lay-people – need specialised training.

8.2.4 Those in formation programmes should have reasonable access to counsellors. Those responsible for formation should be informed, with the candidates' permission, of any factors which become apparent during counselling which would have a bearing on their suitability for the priesthood or religious life.[29]

8.2.5 The placement of candidates for the priesthood or religious life in pastoral work, in such places as residential homes or youth clubs, as well as any voluntary work which they undertake, requires careful planning, supervision and assessment. The purpose of any placement must be clearly identified. Candidates must expect and receive the same formal supervision as other trainee staff. Such placements allow those responsible for formation to observe and assess the ability of candidates to relate to those to whom they will be expected to minister. Facilitating candidates to reflect on their pastoral work experience and to learn from it is intrinsic to the formation process.

8.2.6 Since candidates for the priesthood and religious life are being prepared for ministries in which they will be in a position of sacred trust in regard to children, they must be made aware of what are appropriate boundaries in relating to children and of the absolute importance of respecting these boundaries.

---

28. *Pastores Dabo Vobis,* n. 66.
29. Cf. 8.1.5. See c. 220 and c. 642.

## 8.3 Ongoing Formation

*The complex emotional and social nature of priestly and religious ministry in present-day Ireland requires a deepening of faith, a renewal of commitment and a readiness to examine existing approaches to ministry among priests and religious. In-service formation is the best way to bring about the necessary change. An individual's personal growth and fidelity to his or her ministry requires ongoing formation.*[30]

8.3.1  Since a genuine spirituality is central to all personal life, good spiritual direction and counselling are invaluable for priests and religious. Serious personal inadequacies can hide behind questionable spirituality. Ongoing education promoting psycho-sexual maturity, healthy living and human wholeness is essential. Good practice guidelines should be developed in order to promote awareness of the need for appropriate pastoral boundaries.

8.3.2  A pastoral priority for bishops and religious superiors should be to meet individually, on a regular basis, each priest of the diocese or religious of the congregation.

8.3.3  To assist priests and religious in maintaining their spiritual, physical and mental health, and to facilitate their ongoing education and formation, they should be encouraged to undertake sabbatical programmes at intervals during their ministries – for example, after ten and/or twenty-five years of ministry.

8.3.4  Dynamic leadership of the Christian community increasingly demands greater collaboration between bishops, priests, religious and lay people. For such collaborative ministry to become effective, priority needs to be given to adult religious education programmes in which each person in the Church can be offered the possibility and challenge of ongoing formation.

---

30. *Pastores Dabo Vobis*, n. 70.

# Chapter 9

# Towards Greater Awareness of the Problem of Child Sexual Abuse

## 9.1 Context

9.1.1 The prevention of child sexual abuse, the creation of an atmosphere which enables the victims of abuse to disclose what has happened to them, and the quality of the response made by those to whom disclosure is made, are all significantly influenced by the level of awareness and understanding of the issue of child sexual abuse among the public in general and among those occupying leadership roles in the community.

9.1.2 Despite the degree to which media and public attention has focused on child sexual abuse in recent times, there still remains a significant degree of denial of the problem, with many people having difficulty accepting the occurrence of such abuse and its presence in all strata of society. Moreover, even if there is acknowledgement that the problem exists and is widespread, people may be unaware of how they should appropriately respond when faced with an actual situation of child sexual abuse.

9.1.3 Thus, there is a need to facilitate increased awareness and better-informed attitudes regarding the multi-faceted issues surrounding child sexual abuse.

9.1.4 There needs to be widespread dissemination of basic information on the nature of child sexual abuse; its effects on victims; the behaviour patterns of abusers; and the need for therapeutic help for victims, abusers and others affected. In addition, there needs to be awareness and understanding of guidelines on action to be taken in situations where abuse is suspected. In order to fulfil these needs, it is necessary that education programmes be devised and implemented at local level.

9.1.5    While Church authorities must consider how they can contribute generally to this process of education and awareness-raising, they must focus especially on fulfilling their responsibilities in respect of:

- priests and religious;

- those working with children and young people in educational or other institutions run or managed by the Church;

- those occupying leadership positions within Church organisations.

## 9.2    Proposals

9.2.1    Priests and religious should receive ongoing education and in-service training in regard to the nature and effects of child sexual abuse. This is necessary to ensure that they reach out with competence and compassion to all victims of child sexual abuse whom they encounter in the course of their ministry. Furthermore, such education and training should help towards ensuring that proper procedures for the protection of children are put in place in respect of all institutions they are involved in managing – schools, youth facilities, for example.

9.2.2    It is recommended that information days or seminars on child sexual abuse continue to be arranged for priests and religious. These information days and seminars should be followed up by the provision of new and additional information as and when it becomes available. It would be particularly appropriate if practitioners from the health authorities, the police, and other professional bodies were contributors to this educational process.

9.2.3    Through the information days and seminars mentioned, and through other means, information about policies and procedures in regard to child sexual abuse in force from statutory and Church sources should be disseminated, so that these policies and procedures are known, clearly understood, and their implications fully appreciated. Priests and religious need to be alerted to the necessary links between their role and that of the agencies with statutory obligations for the protection of children.

9.2.4 Education in the area of child sexual abuse needs to be provided on an ongoing basis to all involved in the formation of students to the priesthood and religious life.

9.2.5 Candidates for the priesthood and religious life need to continue to be made aware of the nature of child sexual abuse and its effects on victims and their families. In the course of their future ministry they may well come across situations of child sexual abuse, and so it is important to help them gain knowledge as to how to respond properly to these. Particular attention should be paid to the issue of child sexual abuse by priests and religious. Candidates should be made aware of the implications and consequences of this in civil law and in canon law and of the procedures for dealing with it.

9.2.6 In so far as the Church holds managerial responsibility for schools, it should provide, or assist in providing, information days for teachers and school boards of management in co-operation with education authorities and teachers' unions, and involving the health authorities, the police, and other professionals as appropriate.

9.2.7 There is need for school-based programmes for children and young people designed to enable them become aware of their right to say 'No' to certain behaviour on the part of adults. The programmes should also help children and young people understand that they have a right to tell if they have cause to fear certain adults, and to disclose if they have suffered abuse. Such programmes need to be developed in the light of emerging information and out of the experience gained from those currently in use.

9.2.8 The Church should co-operate with others in providing education for the general public on child sexual abuse. Those responsible for adult religious education at diocesan level should consider what they might contribute in this area.

## Organisations Represented at the Listening Days held by the Advisory Committee

The following statutory and voluntary agencies contributed to the listening days held by the Advisory Committee during January and February 1995:

Barnardo's

Council for the Status of Women (now National Women's Council of Ireland)

Department of Health

Department of Health and Social Services, Northern Ireland

Dublin Rape Crisis Centre

Garda Síochána (Domestic Violence and Sexual Assault Investigation Unit)

Irish Association of Social Workers

Irish Society for the Prevention of Cruelty to Children

National Parents Council (Primary)

Resident Managers Association

RUC

Support Network for Professionals in Child Protection

Support Network for Survivors

# The Law Relating to Reporting of Child Sexual Abuse

## The Law in the Republic of Ireland

The present statutory framework does not make mandatory the reporting of incidents of child sexual abuse to either the health board or Garda Síochána. Accordingly, there is no statutory obligation on any person to report child sexual abuse or suspicions of child sexual abuse.

The criminal law does contain a little-known and seldom-used offence called 'misprision of felony', which punishes failure to report the commission of offences categorised as felonies, which include rape and buggery. Many of the offences relevant in the context of child sexual abuse are not felonies and, accordingly, misprision is of limited relevance.

Nevertheless, as outlined in Appendix 3, guidelines on child sexual abuse were issued by the Department of Health in 1987 and again in 1995, the latter jointly with the Gardaí. These guidelines provide a framework for the reporting and investigation of suspicions of child sexual abuse. It is understood that the Department of Health proposes to publish a discussion paper on the issue of mandatory reporting in the near future.

## The Law in Northern Ireland

The law in Northern Ireland was the same as the law in the Republic of Ireland until 1967 when the Criminal Law Act (NI) was passed. It was an Act intended to abolish the division of crimes into felonies and misdemeanours. Section 2 (i) of that Act created a new offence, an 'arrestable offence', being any offence for which the Court can by law sentence the offender to imprisonment for a term of five years or more, including attempts to commit any such offence.

Section 5 of the Act provides:
*where a person has committed an arrestable offence, it shall be the duty of every other person, who knows or believes:*

*(a)      that the offence or some other arrestable offence has been committed;*

*and*

*(b)      that he has information which is likely to secure, or to be of material assistance in securing, the apprehension, prosecution or conviction of any person for that offence to give that information, within a reasonable time, to a Constable and if, without reasonable excuse, he fails to do so he shall be guilty of an offence ...*

Most cases of child sexual abuse fall within the category of arrestable offences. Since 1861 it has been an offence, punishable by up to ten years imprisonment, to commit an indecent assault on a male. Until 1989 such an offence against a female carried only a maximum of two years imprisonment but that was increased to ten years. However, certain sexual offences against children, including gross indecency, are not arrestable offences and there is no obligation imposed by law to report these.

It should be noted that, where the obligation to report exists, the report must be *to a constable.*

What constitutes a reasonable excuse is a question of fact in each individual case.

# Legal Framework

Both parts of Ireland have ratified the United Nations Convention on the Rights of the Child. Article 19 of the Convention obliges subscribing states to take all appropriate legislative, administrative, social and educational measures to protect children from abuse or exploitation, including sexual abuse. Clause 2 of that Article states that:

> *Such protective measures should, as appropriate, include effective procedures for the establishment of social programmes to provide necessary support for the child and for those who have the care of the child, as well as for other forms of prevention and for identification, reporting, referral, investigation, treatment and follow-up of instances of child maltreatment described heretofore, and, as appropriate, for judicial involvement.*[31]

The fact that the Convention has been ratified does not mean that it forms part of the law of the country. However, both parts of Ireland have a binding obligation under international law to ensure that the terms of the treaty are honoured.

## Republic of Ireland

The duty of investigating criminal offences in the Republic of Ireland is vested by law in the Garda Síochána. It must be remembered that in a criminal trial the benefit of any doubt will be given to the accused. This is expressed in the principle that the accused is presumed innocent until proven guilty and in the heavy onus that is placed on the prosecution to prove its case beyond reasonable doubt. The operation of this principle means that, in cases of doubt, guilty persons may sometimes be acquitted.

---

31. The text of the Convention is contained in many publications including *The Rights of the Child*, Geneva: United Nations, 1990, Human Rights Fact Sheets Series, No. 10, pp. 13-32, and The Council for Social Welfare, *The Rights of the Child: Irish Perspectives on the UN Convention*, Dublin: The Council for Social Welfare, 1991, pp. 93-122.

Under statute, responsibility for the identification of children who are suspected of having been sexually abused or who are at risk of sexual abuse is vested in the health boards.

Each health board is statutorily required to promote the welfare of children in its area who are not receiving adequate care and protection. Section 3 (2) of the Child Care Act 1991 provides:

*In the performance of this function, a health board shall –*

(a)     *take such steps as it considers requisite to identify children who are not receiving adequate care and protection and co-ordinate information from all relevant sources relating to children in its area;*

(b)     *having regard to the rights and duties of parents, whether under the Constitution or otherwise –*

     (i)     *regard the welfare of the child as the first and paramount consideration, and*

     (ii)     *in so far as is practicable, give due consideration, having regard to his age and understanding, to the wishes of the child; and*

(c)     *have regard to the principle that it is generally in the best interests of the child to be brought up in his own family.*

In 1987 the Department of Health issued the revised *Guidelines on Procedures for the Identification, Investigation and Management of Child Abuse.* These guidelines pre-date the statutory obligation of health boards in regard to the identification of children at risk. The guidelines outline a procedure in which the Director of Community Care is charged with responsibility for monitoring and co-ordinating the management of allegations of child sexual abuse.

Following the present restructuring in the health boards, the function of the Director of Community Care in relation to child sexual abuse will become the responsibility of a named designated officer of each board.

Further guidelines, *Notification of Suspected Cases of Child Abuse Between Health Boards and Gardaí*, were issued jointly by the Department of Health and the Gardaí in 1995. This document amends the 1987 guidelines in relation to the circumstances in which the health boards and the Gardaí are to notify suspected cases of child abuse to each other, and in relation to the consultations which should take place between both agencies following a notification. They provide for a co-ordinated approach on the part of the health boards and the Gardaí, recognising and respecting their different roles and responsibilities in child abuse cases.

In the exercise of their responsibilities, both health boards and the Gardaí are governed by the Constitution. Of particular relevance in the area of child sexual abuse are those articles of the Constitution which outline the rights of the family, of parents and of children.[32] A Church response to child sexual abuse by priests and religious must also be respectful of these rights.

## Northern Ireland

The relevant legislation dealing with the welfare of children and young persons in Northern Ireland is the Children and Young Persons Act (NI) 1968. A child is there defined as a person under the age of fourteen years and a young person means a person who has attained the age of fourteen years but is under the age of seventeen years (Section 185).

Under Article 17(i) of the Health and Personal Social Services (NI) Order 1972, the Department of Health and Social Services has directed health and social services boards to exercise on its behalf certain functions with regard to the administration of the health and personal social services. Such functions include the child protection duties contained in the Children and Young Persons Act (NI) 1968. That Act imposes a responsibility on boards to investigate any case where there is information to suggest that a child may be at risk and to take appropriate action to protect that child and to promote the child's welfare. This responsibility applies to all children in the community, whether they are living at home with their parents, living with other carers or living in a residential setting.

---

32. Cf. Article 41.1, Article 42.1 and Article 42.5.

Health and social services boards have a specific duty to investigate situations where it is believed that a child is at risk and that grounds for bringing care proceedings may exist. That duty is described in Section 94 (ii) of the 1968 Act:

(ii)     *For the purposes of (I) if the Department (Board) receives information suggesting that any child or young person may be in need of care, protection or control it shall be the duty of the Department (Board) to cause enquiries to be made into the case unless it is satisfied that such enquiries are unnecessary.*

Section 103 (I) of the same 1968 Act states:

1.     *Where it appears to a Department (a Board) with respect to a child appearing to it to be under the age of seventeen years —*

     (a)   *that he has neither parent nor guardian or has been and remains abandoned by his parents or guardians or is lost;*

     *or*

     (b)   *that his parents or guardian are, for the time being or permanently, prevented by reason of mental or bodily disease or infirmity or other incapacity or in any other circumstances from providing for his proper accommodation, maintenance and upbringing;*

     *and in either case, that the intervention of the Department (the Board) under this Section is necessary in the interests of the welfare of the child, it shall be the duty of the Department (the Board) to receive the child into its care under this Section.*

The general duty of boards to promote the welfare of children is described in Section 164 of the 1968 Act:

(i)     *It shall be the duty of the Department (Board) to make available such advice, guidance and assistance as may promote the welfare of children by diminishing the need to receive children into or keep them in care under this Act or to bring children before a Court; and any provisions made by the Department (Board) under this subsection may, if the Department (Board) think fit, include provision for giving assistance in kind or, in exceptional circumstances, in cash.*

Following the publication of the Report of the Cleveland Inquiry[33] the Department of Health and Social Services in Northern Ireland published *Co-operating to Protect Children: A Guide for Health and Social Services Boards in the Management of Child Abuse* in December 1989. A circular, HSS (CC) 4/89, was issued at the same time. These were intended to implement the recommendations of the Cleveland Report and emphasised the need for close co-operation between the various statutory agencies with the welfare of the child, including the police, underlined the necessity for training of the personnel involved and proposed, *inter alia,* that each board should regularly review and, if necessary, revise the guidelines contained in its local procedural handbooks.

A supplement to circular HSS (CC) 4/89 was issued on 31 March 1995 following the Health and Personal Social Services (NI) Order 1994. That Order came into effect on 1 April 1994 and enabled boards to delegate the exercise of certain statutory functions to health and social services trusts. These trusts are bound by the same policies and guidance as boards and they have statutory responsibility for the provision of child protection services. Trusts are accountable to the board for the discharge of certain child care functions under the Children and Young Persons Act and they must prepare and agree with the boards schemes relating to those functions. Boards continue to have a general duty to promote the welfare of children under Section 164 of the Act but services under this section are provided by the trusts on a contractual basis.

The 1968 Act will be largely repealed by the Children (NI) Order 1995 which is being introduced from October 1996. The current DHSS guidance contained in *Co-operating to Protect Children* and the two circulars are under review to take account of that. The Children (NI) Order 1995 abolishes the distinction between children and young persons.

---

33. Elizabeth Butler-Sloss, *Report of the Inquiry into Child Sexual Abuse in Cleveland 1987,* London: HMSO, 1988.

Article Two of the Order defines a child as a person under the age of eighteen years.

The police are involved in cases of child abuse as a consequence of their general responsibility for the protection of life, the prevention and investigation of crime and the submission of cases for criminal proceedings. In addition, the police have a number of protective functions in relation to children under the 1968 Act. As with health and social services boards and the NSPCC, they have a power to bring children and young people in need of care, protection or control before a juvenile court and they have emergency powers, not available to other agencies, to detain a child in a place of safety without prior application to a court or a justice of the peace. Where speed is essential to protect a child they can enter premises without a warrant (Article 19 (i) (e) of the Police and Criminal Evidence (NI) Order 1989).

# Sample Form for a System of Formal Referencing

REQUEST FOR PERMISSION TO MINISTER
IN THE DIOCESE OF ........................

I, ................................... (Name of Bishop/Superior), hereby state that ................................. (Name of title of Applicant) is a Priest/Deacon/Religious of good character and reputation in the ................................. (Name of Diocese or Congregation) and that he/she is qualified to perform pastoral work in an effective and suitable manner in the Diocese of .................................

There is nothing in his/her background that might suggest that he/she would be unsuitable for working with minors. He/she does not have any continuing alcohol or substance abuse problem.

There is no reason in civil law or canon law for his/her leaving his/her present appointment.

I recommend ................................. for pastoral ministry in the Diocese of ................................. and I hereby present him/her for appointment.

DIOCESAN SEAL

Signature: .................................
Bishop/Religious Superior
............................. Date ...........................
Print/Type Postal Address

*On receipt of this completed document, personal verification of the attestation should be sought before accepting the applicant for ministry.*

## GRANT OF PERMISSION

In the light of the above recommendation from .................................... I, .......................................... Bishop of .........................................., hereby accept ....................................... for appointment in the Diocese of ......................................... from ......................................

DIOCESAN SEAL

Signed ....................................................................
Date ...............................

## AGREEMENT OF APPLICANT

I, ................................................. (type/print name of Applicant) hereby confirm that the information I have given to my Bishop/Superior is correct. Furthermore, I confirm that I am willing to accept an appointment for pastoral work from the Bishop of ......................................... and I agree to comply with local Diocesan regulations.

Signed ...................................................................
Date ...............................

# Select Bibliography

*Away from Home and Safe: A Code of Good Practice,* Belfast: North Belfast Community Development Association, 1995.

Beckett, R., A. Beech, D. Fisher and A. S. Fordham (eds.), *Community-based Treatment for Sex Offenders: An Evaluation of Seven Treatment Programmes,* London: Home Office Publications Unit, 1994.

Butler-Sloss, Elizabeth, *Report of the Inquiry into Child Sexual Abuse in Cleveland 1987,* London: HMSO, 1988.

Canadian Conference of Catholic Bishops, *Breach of Trust, Breach of Faith: Child Sexual Abuse in the Church and Society,* Materials for Discussion Groups, Ottawa: Canadian Conference of Catholic Bishops, 1992.

Canadian Conference of Catholic Bishops, *From Pain to Hope: Report of the Ad hoc Committee on Child Sexual Abuse,* Ottawa: Canadian Conference of Catholic Bishops, 1992.

The Canon Law Society of Great Britain and Ireland, *The Canon Law, Letter and Spirit: A Practical Guide to the Code of Canon Law,* Dublin: Veritas Publications, 1995.

*Canonical Delicts Involving Sexual Misconduct and Dismissal from the Clerical State,* Washington DC: National Conference of Catholic Bishops, 1995.

The Cardinal's Commission on Clerical Misconduct with Minors, *Report to Joseph Cardinal Bernadin,* Chicago: Archdiocese of Chicago, 1992.

*Child Abuse: Pastoral and Procedural Guidelines, A Report from the Working Party of the Catholic Bishops' Conference of England and Wales on Cases of Sexual Abuse of Children Involving Priests, Religious and Other Church Workers,* London: Catholic Media Office, 1994.

Child Care (NI), *Our Duty to Care: Principles of Good Practice for the Protection of Children,* Belfast: Child Care (NI), 1995.

*The Code of Canon Law,* English translation, prepared by The Canon Law Society of Great Britain and Ireland in association with The Canon Law Society of Australia and New Zealand and The Canadian Canon Law Society, London: Collins Liturgical Publications, 1983.

Congregation for Institutes of Consecrated Life and Societies of Apostolic Life, *Directives on Formation in Religious Institutes*, Rome: Vatican Polyglot Press, 1990.

The Council for Social Welfare, *The Rights of the Child: Irish Perspectives on the UN Convention*, Dublin: The Council for Social Welfare, 1991.

Department of Education, *Procedures for Dealing with Allegations or Suspicions of Child Abuse*, Dublin: Department of Education, 1991.

Department of Health, *Guidelines on Procedures for the Identification, Investigation and Management on Child Abuse* (revised edition), Dublin: Department of Health, 1987.

Department of Health and Social Services, *An Abuse of Trust: The Report of the Social Services Inspectorate Investigation into the Case of Martin Huston*, Belfast: Department of Health and Social Services, 1993.

Department of Health and Social Services, *Co-operating to Protect Children: A Guide for Health and Social Services Boards on the Management of Child Abuse*, Belfast: Department of Health and Social Services, 1989.

Department of Justice, *A Proposal for a Structured Psychological Treatment Programme for Sex Offenders: Discussion Document*, Dublin: Stationery Office, 1993.

Elliott, Michele (ed.), *Female Sexual Abuse of Children*, London: Longman Group, 1993.

Garda Síochána and Department of Health, *Notification of Suspected Cases of Child Abuse between Health Boards and Gardaí*, Dublin: Garda Síochána and Department of Health, 1995.

Hite, Jordan TOR, Sharon Holland IHM and Daniel Ward OSB (eds.), *Religious Institutes, Secular Institutes, Societies of Apostolic Life: A Handbook of Canons 573-746*, Collegeville: Liturgical Press, 1985.

Hollows, Anne (ed.), *Rebuilding Families After Abuse*, London: National Children's Bureau, 1995.

Irish Society for the Prevention of Cruelty to Children, *Protecting Children: A Discussion Document for Teachers on Child Abuse*, Dublin: ISPCC.

*Kilkenny Incest Investigation*, Dublin: Stationery Office, 1993.

The Law Reform Commission, *Consultation Paper on Child Sexual Abuse*, Dublin: The Law Reform Commission, 1989.

The Law Reform Commission, *Report on Child Sexual Abuse*, Dublin: The Law Reform Commission, 1990.

National Youth Federation, *Dealing With Sexual Abuse: Guidelines for Youth Workers*, Dublin: Irish YouthWork Press, 1995.

North Eastern Health Board, *Child Care: Child Protection Guidelines*, 1994.

*The Report of the Archdiocesan Comission of Enquiry into the Sexual Abuse of Children by Members of the Clergy,* St John's, Newfoundland: Archdiocese of St John's, 1990.
 – Volume One: *Report*
 – Volume Two: *Background Studies and Briefs*
 – Volume Three: *Conclusions and Recommendations*

*The Rights of the Child,* Geneva: United Nations, Human Rights Fact Sheets Series, No. 10, 1990.

Vann, Kevin W. and James I. Donlon (eds.), *Roman Replies and CLSA Advisory Opinions 1995,* Washington DC: Canon Law Society of America, 1995.